THE HOUSE THAT MAX BUILT

MAXWELL NEWHOUSE

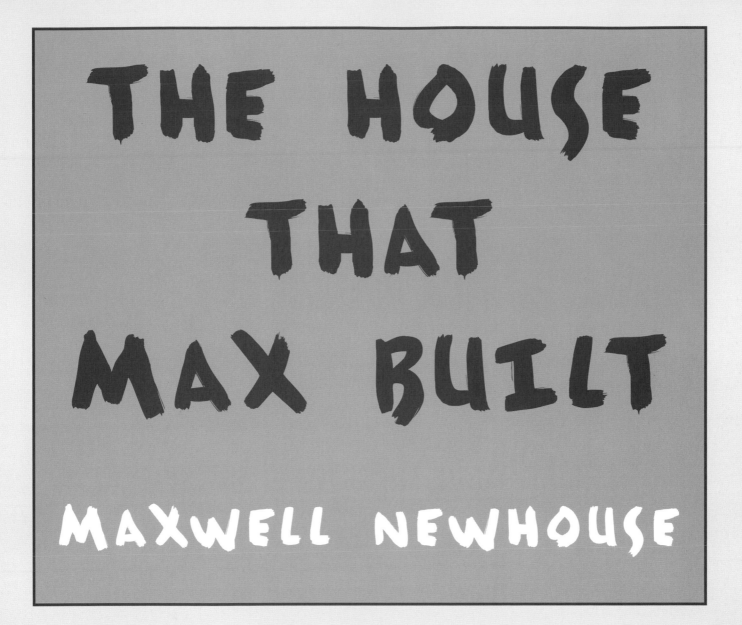

TUNDRA BOOKS

Published in Canada by Tundra Books,
75 Sherbourne Street, Toronto, Ontario M5A 2P9

Published in the United States by Tundra Books of Northern New York,
P.O. Box 1030, Plattsburgh, New York 12901

Library of Congress Control Number: 2007927436

Library and Archives Canada Cataloguing in Publication

Newhouse, Maxwell
    The house that Max built / Maxwell Newhouse.

For ages 4-7.
ISBN 978-0-88776-774-6

    1. House construction – Juvenile literature. I. Title.

TH4811.5.N49 2008   j690'.8   C2007-902731-8

We acknowledge the financial support of the Government of Canada through the Book Publishing Industry
Development Program (BPIDP) and that of the Government of Ontario through the Ontario Media Development
Corporation's Ontario Book Initiative. We further acknowledge the support of the Canada Council for the Arts
and the Ontario Arts Council for our publishing program.

ONTARIO ARTS COUNCIL
CONSEIL DES ARTS DE L'ONTARIO

Medium: Oil on canvas

Design: Leah Springate

Printed in China

1 2 3 4 5 6   13 12 11 10 09 08

TO MY DARLING WIFE, LILLIAN

ACKNOWLEDGMENTS

Thank you to Richmond School District #38 for their support.
A special thank-you to the staff and students of James Whiteside Elementary School.

Max wants to build a house beside the lake. He needs a lot of help.

The architect draws up the plans and shows them to Max and the contractor.

The first crew brings an excavator to clear the site where the house will stand. "I want a view of the lake," says Max.

Once the site is level, it is time to lay the cement foundation.
"I will need a basement," says Max.

Next comes the framing crew. They build a floor frame to hold the house.

The framing crew puts the walls together on the floor and then raises them into place. "It's beginning to look like a house," says Max.

Max helps the crew make the roof frame. "There are many kinds of roofs to choose from," he says, "and I want one that keeps out the rain and snow."

After the crew erects the porch frame, they join Max for a picnic lunch in the crisp air.

"Every house needs windows and doors," says Max. The crew follows the plans to place the windows and doors just so, to let the light in and make the house comfortable.

The frame of the house needs to be covered with brick or siding or stone or stucco.
"It's brick for me," says Max. He watches the bricklayers spread the mortar.

Now Max chooses the covering for the roof. "I want shingles," he says to the roofers. "Green, please."

Max is happy to see the plumber. Houses need ways to bring water in and out, for cooking, drinking, bathing, laundry, and flushing the toilet.

The electrician installs the wiring, which will bring power safely to the whole house.
Soon the building inspector will come to approve all the work.

Insulation will keep Max's house cozy and save energy.

Outside, the house looks finished, but the drywall still needs to be installed so the walls in Max's house will be smooth and beautiful.

Now the painters arrive to paint each room the exact colors Max chooses.

Next, the tile setter lays tiles in the kitchen and bathroom, while wooden floors
and carpets are laid through the rest of the house.

The cabinets and counters are put in place, then the plumber comes back to install the sinks and tub and toilet.

At last it's time for the gardener to help Max lay out his garden.
"We'll soon be finished," says Max.

Now Max has a new house!

THE PEOPLE WHO HELPED MAX AND WHAT THEY DO

Architect: designs the house and makes the plans

Contractor: organizes the trades and oversees the construction

Equipment Operator: digs out the foundation with an excavator

Cement-Truck Driver: delivers the large truck full of cement

Pump Trucker: pours the cement from the truck into the construction forms

Cement Finisher: smoothes the cement to a nice flat surface

Carpenter: saws the wood and hammers the nails to frame the house

Laborer: fetches the supplies and tidies the construction site

Glazer: cuts the glass for the windows and doors

Bricklayer: builds the fireplace, outside walls, and chimney with bricks and mortar

Roofer: nails the roofing material onto the roof of the house

Plumber: runs the water lines and sewer pipes, then installs the fixtures

Electrician: wires the house for lights, plugs, and switches

Tinsmith: cuts and bends the sheet metal for furnace ducts and vents

Building Inspector: makes sure all the trades are doing their jobs to code

Insulator: places the insulation in the ceilings and walls

Drywaller: cuts and places the wallboard on the ceilings and inside walls

Filler: applies white plaster over the joints in the wallboard and sands it

Tile Setter: sets the tiles with glue and grout on the floors, counters, or walls

Floor Layer: places wood or linoleum on the floors

Painter: paints the house, inside and out

Cabinetmaker: builds and installs the kitchen and bathroom cabinets

Gardener: landscapes the yard with plants, trees, grass, and stones

Free Spirits 'in the Sky

Text and photographs by

John Christopher Fine

Atheneum   1994   New York

Maxwell Macmillan Canada
Toronto

Maxwell Macmillan International
New York   Oxford   Singapore   Sydney

ATHENEUM
Macmillan Publishing Company
866 Third Avenue
New York, NY 10022

MAXWELL MACMILLAN CANADA, INC.
1200 Eglinton Avenue East
Suite 200
Don Mills, Ontario M3C 3N1

Macmillan Publishing Company is part of the Maxwell Communication Group of Companies.

First edition

Printed in Singapore
10   9   8   7   6   5   4   3   2   1
The text of this book is set in Stempel Schneidler.
Book design by Crowded House Design

Library of Congress Cataloging-in-Publication Data

Fine, John Christopher.
Free spirits in the sky: text and photographs / by John Christopher Fine.—1st ed.
p.   cm.
Summary: Provides information about the history and enjoyment of hot air ballooning and an account of an early morning flight.
ISBN 0–689–31705–0
1. Ballooning—Juvenile works.   2. Balloons—Juvenile works.
[1. Hot air balloons.   2. Ballooning.]   I. Title.
GV762.F56   1994
797.5'1—dc20   92-33443

Hot air rises. Everyone has seen smoke from a fire spiraling upward, carrying pieces of paper, leaves, or bits of debris with it. In a heated house, you can tell that warmer air rises by touching the floor and then the much warmer ceiling. Capturing the rising hot air in an envelope is the simple principle of hot-air ballooning. Today's technological improvements have made hot-air ballooning a lot easier than it was in the first experimental flights.

History tells of Chinese tricksters who heated eggshells over candles. They amazed onlookers with their magic by sending the heated shells soaring into the air. This was around 200 B.C. Bartolomeu de Gusmao is said to have demonstrated a hot-air balloon to King John V of Portugal in 1709.

During the eighteenth century, the Montgolfier brothers observed smoke rising and at first assumed smoke was the important thing, not the hot air. It took many smelly fires and a lot of experimentation for them to realize that heating the air inside a paper-and-cloth envelope would cause it to lift off the ground and even carry weight aloft with it.

On September 19, 1783, in Paris, King Louis XVI and Queen Marie Antoinette watched the Montgolfiers' first hot-air balloon rise with passengers: a rooster, a sheep, and a duck. It was a large envelope, forty-one feet in diameter and fifty-seven feet high. The flight lasted eight minutes and covered a distance of two miles. The balloon soared to an altitude of fifteen hundred feet. When the animals landed safely, the next step was to send humans aloft.

The French king then nominated Jean-François Pilâtre de Rozier and Marquis François d'Arlandes for the first manned flight. Pilâtre de Rozier was a French physicist; Arlandes, a nobleman and soldier. Both men began work with the Montgolfier brothers to build a new hot-air balloon.

The manned hot-air balloon flight carried these two pioneers aloft for twenty-five minutes. The men flew five miles across Paris.

Since the first launching of the Montgolfier brothers' balloon in Paris, balloons have crossed the Atlantic; visited frozen reaches of the Arctic; served in warfare; and have been used for meteorological and scientific research, transportation, and in sport for plain enjoyment. Weekend adventurers thrill to low-altitude hot-air balloon flights borne aloft by these free spirits of the sky.

These lighter-than-air ships fall into three general categories: balloons, blimps, and dirigibles. Hot-air balloons consist of an envelope open at the bottom. Air inside the envelope is heated to make the balloon rise. There are also hydrogen- and helium-filled balloons where the gas is contained in an enclosed envelope. Like hot-air balloons, gas balloons move at the mercy of the wind.

Blimps consist of an enclosed envelope filled with helium gas. The gas takes the shape of the outer skin of the blimp. Dirigibles, or zeppelins, are intricate airships containing gas cells within an outer skin built around a rigid framework. Dirigibles and blimps are motored airships borne aloft by their gases, steered and directed by motors and controls affixed to the structures. They are complex, as different from simple hot-air balloons as a large truck might be from a bicycle .

Preparations for Flight

Preparations for a hot-air balloon flight begin before dawn. Crews wake early in the morning to ready the balloons for launching with the first light, when the air is still. When a launch site is chosen, pilots and crew send aloft a red *piball*. *Piball* stands for *pi*lot-inflated *ball*oon. This small balloon is filled with helium from a small tank kept handy. As it rises, pilots can check the speed and direction of the winds at different altitudes. Weather conditions at the launch site must be calm for takeoff, with no turbulence or storms aloft. The best times are early morning and evening—before and after the sun's rays have created enough warmth to produce turbulence near the ground. At these times the surrounding air is cooler as well, meaning that the hot air inside the balloon will have greater lifting ability. In most countries balloons are allowed to fly only in daylight. Special permission and lights are required for night flights.

Once a decision to launch is made, pilots and crew work quickly to set up the equipment. The balloon envelope, made of nylon or Dacron, is pulled from its canvas bag and spread out on the ground. The wicker basket is tilted on its side, facing the unraveled balloon envelope. Most balloonists prefer wicker for their baskets. The woven wooden twigs are flexible, absorb shocks on landing, and can be easily repaired. Passengers and pilot share the basket with propane tanks, ropes, and controls.

As the pilot hooks up cables, attaching the basket to the envelope, a crew member starts a gasoline-powered fan. On signal, once the balloon is properly laid out and connected to the hooks on the basket supports, a crew member goes to the crown, or top, of the balloon and holds the crown line out straight so the balloon will inflate properly. The fan is started and its airstream is directed into the mouth of the envelope.

Passengers or volunteers work together to hold the envelope open. As the envelope begins to take shape on the ground, the pilot checks the parachute top and rip top at the balloon's crown. The parachute top of a balloon can be opened during flight to control altitude and can be reseated and closed again, like a plug in a bathtub. The rip top is connected with Velcro and ring fasteners. When the rip top is pulled, the hot air will rush out and the balloon will deflate very quickly. Rip tops are not used in flight but at landing when high winds are encountered and the pilot wants to deflate quickly to prevent wind damage to the balloon.

When a balloon is partially inflated with air from the mechanical fan, the pilot returns to the basket. The propane in high-pressure tanks in the basket is turned on and the pilot light ignited. Pilot lights in older balloons are ignited by handheld strikers; newer ones have built-in strikers similar to those on new gas stoves. When everything is ready, the pilot orders the crew out of the way. With the bottom of the balloon envelope still held open by the fan's airstream, the propane gas flames are aimed into the opening.

A loud *whoosh* means the propane burners have ignited. A propane burner can give off twenty million British thermal units (BTUs) of heat. Many of the larger balloons have three or four burners to produce sixty million to eighty million BTUs of heat. A home heating unit, by comparison, gives off 150 to 500

BTUs. The pilot must direct the burners carefully so that flames do not destroy the lower balloon fabric. As air inside is heated to around two hundred degrees Fahrenheit, the envelope takes shape, righting the basket as it rises. The burners are mounted on a metal bracket above the basket. A gimbal, or swivel, enables the pilot to swing and tilt the burners as the balloon is being inflated. When the balloon is inflated and rights itself, the pilot swings the gimbal so that the burners end up pointing straight overhead. The flames are now directed upward into the inflated balloon envelope. Crew members jump on the sides of the basket as the balloon rises, to hold it down while passengers scramble aboard. Sometimes the pilot removes one of the propane tanks used for inflating to lighten the basket and make more room for passengers.

The propane tanks used in flight are stainless steel or aluminum. Each tank may hold from ten to thirty gallons of liquid propane. Buddy Bombard, one of the world's foremost hot-air balloon pioneers and pilots, uses 128-foot-tall balloons equipped with three main burners plus a "cow" burner. The cow burner has a bright orange flame and makes less noise than the main burners, allowing for a quieter flight. Cow burners get their name because their softer sound doesn't scare farm animals on the ground. More than one balloonist has been met upon landing by a pitchfork-wielding farmer demanding payment for broken fences or injured animals.

Most balloons have nylon envelopes. Nylon fabric costs about half as much as Dacron but has less heat tolerance—with an outside limit of around 250 degrees Fahrenheit, compared with Dacron's 325-degree limit. Dacron fabric will last for some six hundred hours of balloon flight, while nylon will last four hundred hours and will shrink 20 percent when exposed to heat. To avoid nylon shrinkage, balloon manufacturers preshrink nylon fabric in an oven at three hundred degrees Fahrenheit. Even balloons with preshrunk nylon fabric lose four feet of surface area over their lifetime.

The lower skirt of a hot-air balloon is made from a heat-and fire-resistant fabric called Nomex. Nomex can absorb radiant heat from the burners without getting brittle. The Nomex skirt goes up about four or five feet, where it is sewn into the nylon or Dacron envelope.

Most hot-air balloons have a scoop. The scoop is a piece of Nomex fabric that comes down as a panel from the skirt to the ring above the basket. The scoop helps funnel air into the envelope and serves to keep crosswinds from blowing out the burners' pilot light.

Balloons usually take off with from sixty to seventy gallons of propane aboard. An average ninety-minute flight burns from fifty to sixty gallons, leaving the pilot with a reserve if the balloon has to lift out of the area where it first lands. This will happen when the pilot finds the pursuit vehicle cannot get to a landing area because of fences or lack of roads.

With everyone aboard, the pilot signals the crew to release the balloon. The pilot blasts the burners again to continue to heat the air inside the envelope.

Flight

Once airborne, a pilot uses the burners to gain altitude. Suddenly, the magic of flight takes over. Heat from the burners drives off the early-morning chill, then silence as the burners are shut off and the balloon glides along, caressed by the gentle wind. Flight is an exciting escape, a time when balloonists can appreciate the wonders of the earth. Aloft, there's time to relax. For about an hour and a half, people enjoy the freedom of flight.

On the ground, crew members pack up quickly and scramble into the launch vehicle. Radios keep the ground crew in contact with the flight crew, but there is no substitute for watching and following a balloon. "Crewing" requires a special skill. A navigator and driver soon find that roads disappear, narrow rutted tracks become impassable, forests suddenly appear in front of them, and villages and fences get in the way of the pursuit vehicle. Airborne, passengers are usually oblivious to all this frantic scrambling. To the aeronauts, people on the ground appear only as small dots on the landscape, occasionally waving or shouting greetings as the balloon dips for a closer look.

21

Passengers and pilots keep a sharp lookout in flight for trees, power lines, other balloons, and even small aircraft. Sometimes a pilot skims so close to trees that passengers can touch the leaves. But when a pilot misjudges by a few inches and comes too close, the wicker basket itself may brush against branches. Other feats taking special skill include touching down in a field, skimming the tops of grain fields, or gently skating close enough over water in a lake or river to cause ripples yet not wet the bottom of the basket.

Although it is difficult to judge the speed of a balloon once it is aloft, instruments can tell a pilot the balloon's rate of ascent or descent in feet per minute and give an exact reading of the balloon's altitude.

Balloon pilots have to develop skills in judging wind currents. At different altitudes air currents may blow from entirely different directions. A hot-air balloon can go up or down, depending on whether the pilot uses the burners to heat the air or vents the air from inside the envelope. There may also be left and right vents built into the sides of the balloon envelope. The pilot can pull a line during flight to open one of these turning vents. The air pressure inside the balloon keeps the slot closed until the line is pulled. Opening the turning vent allows air inside the balloon to shoot out as if through a little jet nozzle. A balloon can be turned left or right, depending on which line the pilot pulls.

Happy Landings

As the propane reserve is reached, the pilot seeks out an appropriate landing site. Finding a spot to land a balloon where the chase crew and vehicle can reach it is often tricky business. Almost every balloonist can tell funny stories about fickle winds that put them into unusual situations. One pilot landed his balloon in a prison yard, only to be confronted by correction

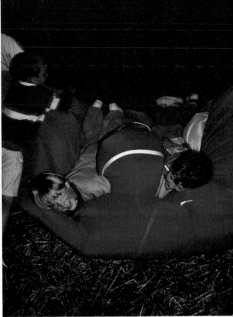

officers armed with machine guns. The guards thought the balloon was part of an elaborate prison escape plot.

When a hot-air balloon lands, it is a lot of work to get all the air out of the envelope and then pack it away. This is where a good recruiter puts onlookers to work. In one field where scores of young people came running to see the balloon land, they were recruited to help fold the nylon envelope. It was all good fun as children, and many of their parents, jumped on the large sprawling nylon to push air out the top. It became a wonderful game, rolling in the billowing fabric, then gathering it up with pilot and crew, and rolling again.

Festivals and Fun

If flying aloft in one balloon sounds like fun, imagine hundreds of balloons in all colors, shapes, and sizes launched at the same time. Ballooning festivals and rallies are organized around the world with public participation always welcome. These gala events often host contests. Balloon pilots vie for prizes, demonstrating their skill and ability.

One of the most popular balloon festivals in the United States, held annually in Reno, Nevada, is known as the Great Reno Balloon Race. Pilots gather with their balloons on a field before dawn breaks over the desert. One of the special features of the Reno Balloon Race is the Dawn Patrol. Organizers obtain special permission to launch balloons in darkness before sunrise. The dry early-morning air is cold before the sun comes up, and preparations in predawn darkness are accompanied by pilots and crews trying to stamp off the chill. The balloons are inflated. Bright orange and blue propane flames light up the field. As balloons take shape, pilots and crew hold them down on the launch site, using cow burners to light up the insides of the envelopes. The result is a spectacular array of color as the bright patterns of the balloons are illuminated from inside.

When the signal is given, the Dawn Patrol balloons take off, their colors and patterns looking like beautiful, intricate Christmas decorations against a velvet sky. Dawn Patrol balloons trail blinking strobe lights so they will be visible to aircraft when the pilot is not firing the burners. Dawn Patrol pilots put on a show lighting the sky above Reno with magnificent glowing balls.

The Great Reno Balloon Race also tests pilots' skills in finding the right air currents to guide them closest to a spot marked on the ground in an event called the Hare and the Hound. In this contest, the "official" balloon takes off from the launch field. Soon after, on signal, the "chase" balloons are launched. The object of this event is for the chase balloons, the hounds, to follow the official balloon, the hare. When the hare lands, its crew marks the spot with a large **X**. The chase pilots are each given a numbered beanbag with a trailing ribbon. They try to drop this bag as close to the crossed lines as possible. The team that drops its bag closest to the center of the **X** wins.

While it sounds easy, it is not. Trying to judge winds at different altitudes to follow the hare's course and then fly over the marked spot takes a great deal of skill. Even when hound pilots get close, they can be blown off the mark at the last moment by an unexpected wind. Sometimes one of the

prizes is a set of keys hung on a pole. A hound pilot able to dip down and grab the keys wins the new car the keys fit.

Malcolm Forbes, the late American millionaire, began a ballooning tradition at his Château de Balleroy in Normandy, France. Balloonists from all over the world come to Balleroy for a weekend of ballooning, fun, and fraternity. The Forbes family members bring out their collection of uniquely shaped balloons, and the event is an international happening as people of all nationalities join together to enjoy the peace and tranquillity of balloon exploration and flight as well as the festivities celebrating happy landings.

Ballooning is a common denominator for peace and goodwill, something Malcolm Forbes understood very well. Using his wonderfully shaped hot-air balloons in the forms of an elephant, sphinx, minaret, macaw, castle, bust of the composer Beethoven, Fabergé egg, and Harley-Davidson motorcycle, Forbes and his team flew goodwill missions over many nations of the world.

There are many happy landings in ballooning. It is more than a sport; it cements goodwill. The pure joy of it, the enthusiasm of young and old, the fraternity, regardless of language, when a balloon comes down from the sky—it is a wonder to experience and an event to behold. "Ballooning is peacemaking," Malcolm Forbes said. Truly it is.

Balloon Feats

The history of hot-air ballooning is filled with stories of daring and personal endurance. On July 11, 1897, Salomon-Auguste Andrée and a small team took off to explore the North Pole by balloon. They took carrier pigeons with them. One carrier pigeon dispatch read ALL WELL ON BOARD. THIS IS OUR THIRD DISPATCH. Then the Andrée expedition disappeared. Two more messages washed ashore in bottles in 1899 and 1900. The explorers were presumed dead. In 1930 an Arctic expedition found the frozen bodies of Andrée and crew member Strindberg. Weeks later the body of a third crew member was located with diaries and photographic plates that showed the last months of the explorers' lives.

Andrée's hydrogen balloon covered some five hundred miles over a sixty-five-hour period but was forced aground by icy conditions five hundred miles from the North Pole. The explorers trekked south, making camp on October 5, 1897. Andrée and his team died from trichinosis, a disease caused by a worm-like parasite, which they contracted from eating polar bear meat.

Balloons were used by Napoléon Bonaparte for reconnaissance flights. They were used to send messages out of the besieged city of Paris during the Franco-Prussian War of 1870–1871. They were also used during the American Civil War to spot artillery and to obtain tactical information on troop movements.

At the Forbes ballooning museum on the grounds of the Château de Balleroy, original items from great balloon feats include the gondola from *Double Eagle II*, which flew across the Atlantic from Presque Isle, Maine, to the Irish coast in five days.

Kassia Leprieur, manager of the Forbes château, recounts that when she asked the transatlantic balloon pilot Ben Abruzzo for something he'd used in his crossing to put in the museum, he told her, "Honey, all I have is what I'm wearing." Abruzzo took

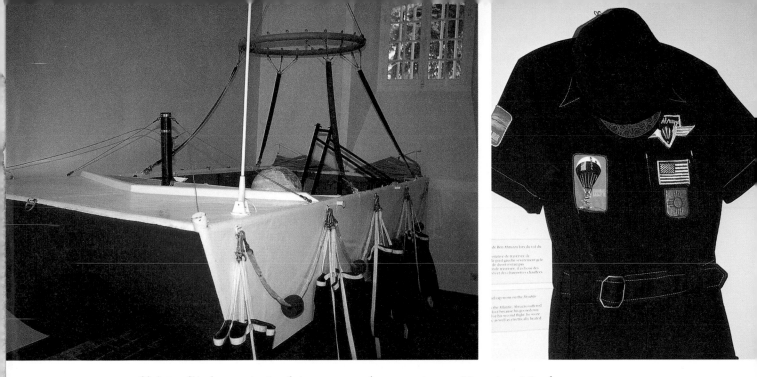

off his flight suit in his car and gave it to Kassia. He later entered his hotel in his shorts.

Whether used by military strategists, explorers, scientists, or sporting enthusiasts, hot-air ballooning remains one of the most thrilling ways to view the earth. A slow flight over spectacular wilderness areas, snow-covered mountains, or sprawling lakes brings feelings of harmony with life itself. Hot-air ballooning remains an adventure, easily shared and safely experienced by thousands of pilots and enthusiasts worldwide.

Balloonists celebrate the conclusion of a flight with a toast and a special prayer. As passengers and crew gather around the wicker basket after landing, the pilot often repeats these words:

May the winds welcome you with softness,
May the sun bless you with his warm hands,
May you fly so high and so well that God joins
   you in laughter and sets you back into
The loving arms of Mother Earth.

In the tradition of ballooning, may your lives be caressed by gentle wind, and may you always have happy landings.